2ND EDITION

PIANO • VOCAL • GUITAR

more of THE BEST SONGS EVER

CONTENTS

ISBN 0-634-00002-0

HAL•LEONARD®
CORPORATION
7777 W. BLUEMOUND RD. P.O. BOX 13819 MILWAUKEE, WI 53213

Visit Hal Leonard Online at
www.halleonard.com

ALFIE
Theme from the Paramount Picture ALFIE

Words by HAL DAVID
Music by BURT BACHARACH

ALL OF ME

Words and Music by SEYMOUR SIMONS
and GERALD MARKS

out you._____ Take my lips_____ I want to

lose them,_____ Take my arms_____

_____ I'll nev-er use them,

Your good-bye_____ left me with eyes that cry,_____

APRIL IN PARIS

Words by E.Y. HARBURG
Music by VERNON DUKE

A-pril's in the air, but here in Par - is

A - pril wears a dif - f'rent gown. You can see her waltz - ing

down the street. The tang of

AUTUMN IN NEW YORK

Words and Music by
VERNON DUKE

AUTUMN LEAVES
(Les Feuilles Mortes)

English lyric by JOHNNY MERCER
French lyric by JACQUES PREVERT
Music by JOSEPH KOSMA

BEAUTY AND THE BEAST
from Walt Disney's BEAUTY AND THE BEAST

Lyrics by HOWARD ASHMAN
Music by ALAN MENKEN

CABARET
from the Musical CABARET

Words by FRED EBB
Music by JOHN KANDER

Energetically

What good is sit - ting a - lone in your room?
Put down the knit - ting, the book and the broom,

Come hear the mu - sic play;
Time for a hol - i - day;

Life is a cab - a - ret, old chum, _ Come to the

BEYOND THE SEA

English Lyrics by JACK LAWRENCE
Music and French Lyrics by CHARLES TRENET

31

CARAVAN
from SOPHISTICATED LADIES

Words and Music by DUKE ELLINGTON,
IRVING MILLS and JUAN TIZOL

CHEEK TO CHEEK
from the RKO Radio Motion Picture TOP HAT

Words and Music by
IRVING BERLIN

COME RAIN OR COME SHINE
from ST. LOUIS WOMAN

Words by JOHNNY MERCER
Music by HAROLD ARLEN

CRY ME A RIVER

Words and Music by
ARTHUR HAMILTON

DESAFINADO
(Off Key)

English Lyric by GENE LEES
Original Text by NEWTON MENDONCA
Music by ANTONIO CARLOS JOBIM

EASY TO LOVE
(You'd Be So Easy to Love)
from BORN TO DANCE

Words and Music by
COLE PORTER

59

Don't cry __ out loud, _____ just keep it in - side, learn how to
Fly high __ and proud, _____ and if you should fall re - mem-ber you

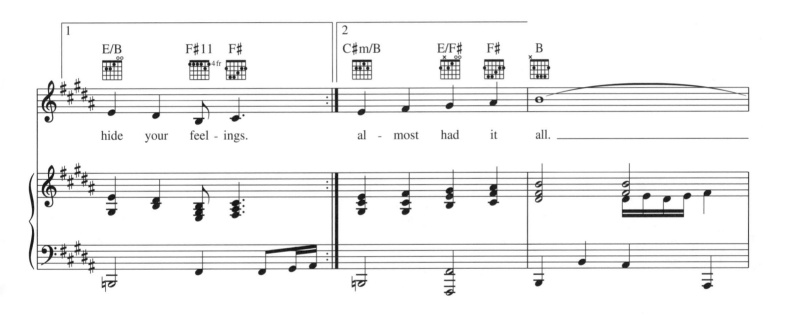

hide your feel - ings.

al - most had it all. _____

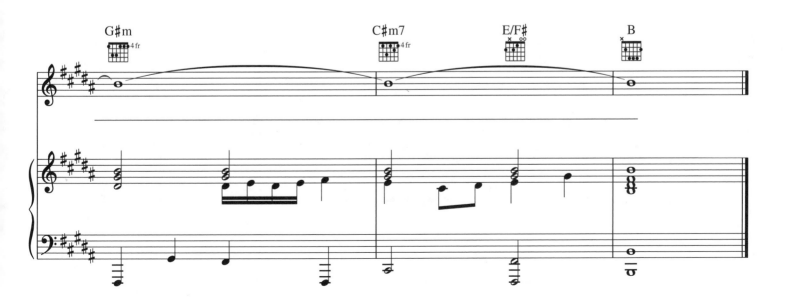

DON'T GET AROUND MUCH ANYMORE

Words and Music by DUKE ELLINGTON
and BOB RUSSELL

EASTER PARADE

featured in the Motion Picture Irving Berlin's EASTER PARADE

Words and Music by
IRVING BERLIN

ENDLESS LOVE

from ENDLESS LOVE

Words and Music by
LIONEL RICHIE

FALLING IN LOVE WITH LOVE
from THE BOYS FROM SYRACUSE

Words by LORENZ HART
Music by RICHARD RODGERS

THE FIRST TIME EVER I SAW YOUR FACE

Words and Music by
EWAN MacCOLL

A FINE ROMANCE
from SWING TIME

Words by DOROTHY FIELDS
Music by JEROME KERN

THE GLORY OF LOVE

Words and Music by
BILLY HILL

90

GOOD MORNING HEARTACHE

Words and Music by DAN FISHER,
IRENE HIGGINBOTHAM and ERVIN DRAKE

GROW OLD WITH ME

Words and Music by
JOHN LENNON

Tenderly

Grow old ___ a - long with me.
___ a - long with me,
___ a - long with me.

The
two
What -

best is yet ___ to be. ___
branch - es of ___ one tree. ___
ev - er fate ___ de - crees, ___

When our time has come, ___
Face the set - ting sun ___
we will see it through, ___

___ we will be as one. ___
___ when the day is done. ___
___ for our love is true. ___

God bless our

I CAN'T GET STARTED WITH YOU

from ZIEGFELD FOLLIES

Words by IRA GERSHWIN
Music by VERNON DUKE

HEART AND SOUL
from the Paramount Short Subject A SONG IS BORN

Words by FRANK LOESSER
Music by HOAGY CARMICHAEL

Moderately, lightly rhythmical

HELLO, YOUNG LOVERS
from THE KING AND I

Lyrics by OSCAR HAMMERSTEIN II
Music by RICHARD RODGERS

110

HEY JUDE

Words and Music by JOHN LENNON
and PAUL McCARTNEY

HOW ARE THINGS IN GLOCCA MORRA

from FINIAN'S RAINBOW

Words by E.Y. HARBURG
Music by BURTON LANE

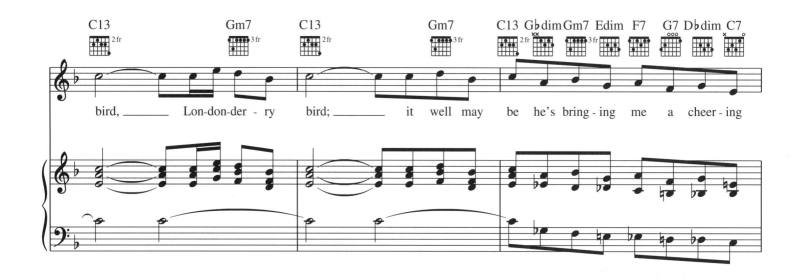

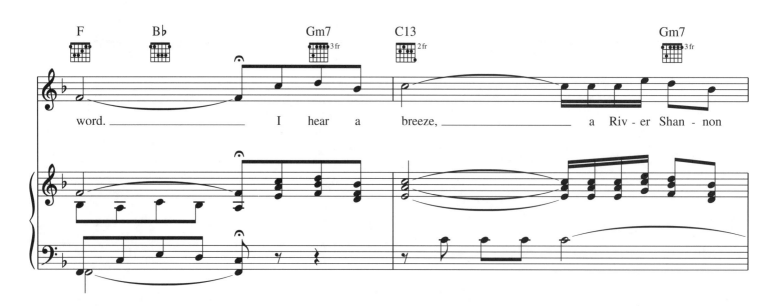

HOW HIGH THE MOON

from TWO FOR THE SHOW

Words by NANCY HAMILTON
Music by MORGAN LEWIS

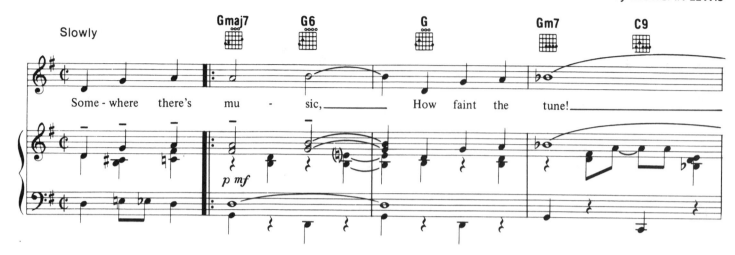

Somewhere there's music, How faint the tune!

Somewhere there's heaven, How High The Moon! There is no

moon above When love is far away too, Till it comes true

I COULD WRITE A BOOK

from PAL JOEY

Words by LORENZ HART
Music by RICHARD RODGERS

I DREAMED A DREAM
from LES MISÉRABLES

Music by CLAUDE-MICHEL SCHÖNBERG
Lyrics by HERBERT KRETZMER
Original Text by ALAIN BOUBLIL and JEAN-MARC NATEL

I HEARD IT
THROUGH THE GRAPEVINE

Words and Music by NORMAN J. WHITFIELD
and BARRETT STRONG

I HONESTLY LOVE YOU

Words and Music by PETER ALLEN
and JEFF BARRY

May-be I hang a-round_ here a lit-tle more than I should; we
You don't_ have to an-swer; I see it in your eyes.

both know I got some-where else_ to go. But
May-be it was bet-ter left_ un-said. But

140

I'VE GOT THE WORLD ON A STRING

Lyric by TED KOEHLER
Music by HAROLD ARLEN

Mer - ry month of May, sun - ny

142

I LOVE PARIS
from CAN-CAN

Words and Music by
COLE PORTER

I'LL REMEMBER APRIL

Words and Music by PAT JOHNSON,
DON RAYE and GENE DE PAUL

Moderately, with expression

I'VE GROWN ACCUSTOMED TO HER FACE

from MY FAIR LADY

Words by ALAN JAY LERNER
Music by FREDERICK LOEWE

IF

Words and Music by
DAVID GATES

IN THE MOOD

By JOE GARLAND

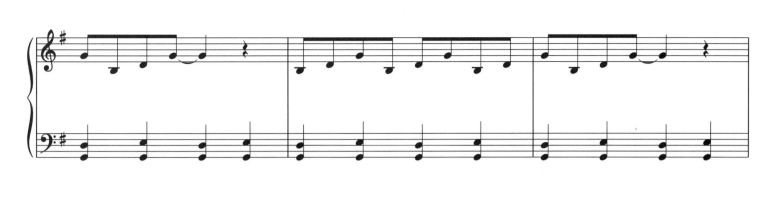

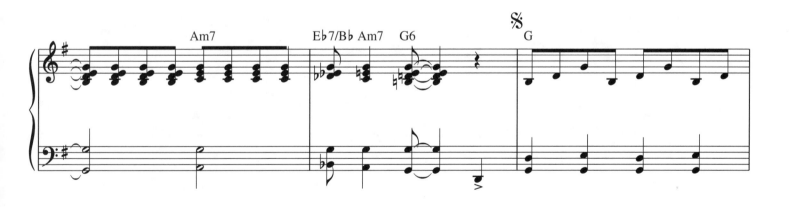

162

IT'S ONLY A PAPER MOON

Lyric by BILLY ROSE and E.Y. HARBURG
Music by HAROLD ARLEN

JUST IN TIME
from BELLS ARE RINGING

Words by BETTY COMDEN and ADOLPH GREEN
Music by JULE STYNE

JUST ONCE

Words by CYNTHIA WEIL
Music by BARRY MANN

169

LITTLE GIRL BLUE
from JUMBO

Words by LORENZ HART
Music by RICHARD RODGERS

Moderately

LULLABY OF BIRDLAND

Words by GEORGE DAVID WEISS
Music by GEORGE SHEARING

MICHELLE

Words and Music by JOHN LENNON
and PAUL McCARTNEY

Mi - chelle, ma belle, these are words that go to - geth - er

well, my Mi - chelle.___ Mi - chelle, ma belle,
Mi - chelle, ma belle,

sont des mots qui vont tres bien en - semble, tres bien en - semble.
sont des mots qui vont tres bien en - semble, tres bien en - semble.

MISTY

Words by JOHNNY BURKE
Music by ERROLL GARNER

Slowly, with expression

MY BLUE HEAVEN

Lyric by GEORGE WHITING
Music by WALTER DONALDSON

MY HEART WILL GO ON
(Love Theme from 'Titanic')
from the Paramount and Twentieth Century Fox Motion Picture TITANIC

Music by JAMES HORNER
Lyric by WILL JENNINGS

MY ROMANCE
from JUMBO

Words by LORENZ HART
Music by RICHARD RODGERS

NATURE BOY

Words and Music by
EDEN AHBEZ

THE NEARNESS OF YOU
from the Paramount Picture ROMANCE IN THE DARK

Words by NED WASHINGTON
Music by HOAGY CARMICHAEL

A NIGHTINGALE SANG IN BERKELEY SQUARE

Lyric by ERIC MASCHWITZ
Music by MANNING SHERWIN

Pronounced "Bar-kley"

OH, WHAT A BEAUTIFUL MORNIN'
from OKLAHOMA!

Lyrics by OSCAR HAMMERSTEIN II
Music by RICHARD RODGERS

RAINDROPS KEEP FALLIN' ON MY HEAD

Lyric by HAL DAVID
Music by BURT BACHARACH

216

ON A CLEAR DAY
(You Can See Forever)
from ON A CLEAR DAY YOU CAN SEE FOREVER

Words by ALAN JAY LERNER
Music by BURTON LANE

RAINY DAYS AND MONDAYS

Lyrics by PAUL WILLIAMS
Music by ROGER NICHOLS

223

D.S. al Coda

ST. LOUIS BLUES

Words and Music by
W.C. HANDY

228

Extra Choruses (optional)

Lawd, a blonde-headed woman makes a good man leave the town,
I said a blonde-headed woman makes a good man leave the town,
But a red-head woman makes a boy slap his papa down.

O ashes to ashes and dust to dust,
I said ashes to ashes and dust to dust,
If my blues don't get you my jazzing must.

SENTIMENTAL JOURNEY

Words and Music by BUD GREEN,
LES BROWN and BEN HOMER

Ev - 'ry roll-ing stone gets to feel a - lone when home, sweet home is far a - way. ____

I'm a roll-ing stone who's been so a - lone un - til to - day.

Gon - na take a sen - ti - men - tal jour-ney, gon - na set my

SOME ENCHANTED EVENING

from SOUTH PACIFIC

Lyrics by OSCAR HAMMERSTEIN II
Music by RICHARD RODGERS

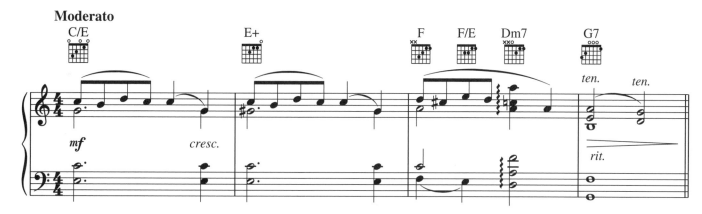

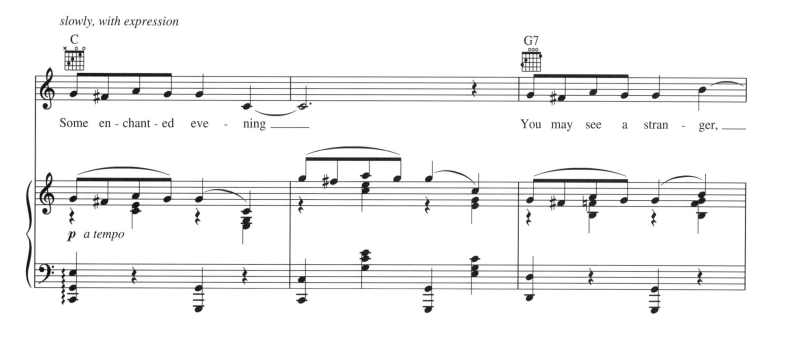

236

SOMETHING

Words and Music by
GEORGE HARRISON

Some-thing in ___ the way ___ she moves, ___
Some-where in ___ her smile ___ she knows, ___
Some-thing in ___ the way ___ she knows, ___

___ at-tracts ___ me like ___ no oth-er ___ lov-er.
___ that I ___ don't need ___ no oth-er ___ lov-er.
___ and all ___ I have ___ to do is think ___ of her.

Some-thing in _ the way _ she woos ___ me. _
Some-thing in _ her style _ that shows ___ me. _
Some-thing in _ the things _ she shows ___ me. _

I don't want to leave _ her now, ___ you

SOPHISTICATED LADY

from SOPHISTICATED LADIES

Words and Music by DUKE ELLINGTON,
IRVING MILLS and MITCHELL PARISH

SOMEWHERE, MY LOVE
Lara's Theme from DOCTOR ZHIVAGO

Lyric by PAUL FRANCIS WEBSTER
Music by MAURICE JARRE

STELLA BY STARLIGHT

from the Paramount Picture THE UNINVITED

Words by NED WASHINGTON
Music by VICTOR YOUNG

TAKE THE "A" TRAIN

Words and Music by
BILLY STRAYHORN

THIS CAN'T BE LOVE
from THE BOYS FROM SYRACUSE

Words by LORENZ HART
Music by RICHARD RODGERS

In Ve-ro-na my late cous-in Ro-me-o _____

Was three times as stu-pid as my Dro-mi-o. _____

For he fell in love and then he died of it, _____

TENDERLY
from TORCH SONG

Lyric by JACK LAWRENCE
Music by WALTER GROSS

THERE'S NO BUSINESS LIKE SHOW BUSINESS

from the Stage Production ANNIE GET YOUR GUN

Words and Music by
IRVING BERLIN

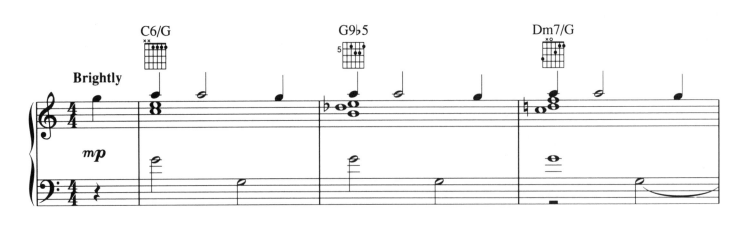

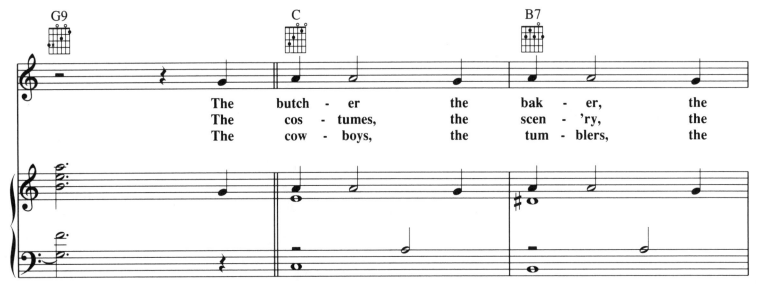

The butch - er the bak - er, the
The cos - tumes, the scen - 'ry, the
The cow - boys, the tum - blers, the

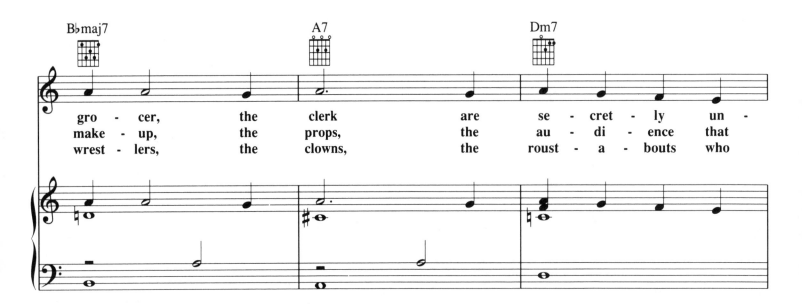

gro - cer, the clerk are se - cret - ly un -
make - up, the props, the au - di - ence that
wrest - lers, the clowns, the roust - a - bouts who

TRY TO REMEMBER
from THE FANTASTICKS

Words by TOM JONES
Music by HARVEY SCHMIDT

THE WAY YOU LOOK TONIGHT

from SWING TIME

Words by DOROTHY FIELDS
Music by JEROME KERN

WHAT A DIFF'RENCE A DAY MADE

English Words by STANLEY ADAMS
Music and Spanish Words by MARIA GREVER

WHAT I DID FOR LOVE

from A CHORUS LINE

Music by MARVIN HAMLISCH
Lyric by EDWARD KLEBAN

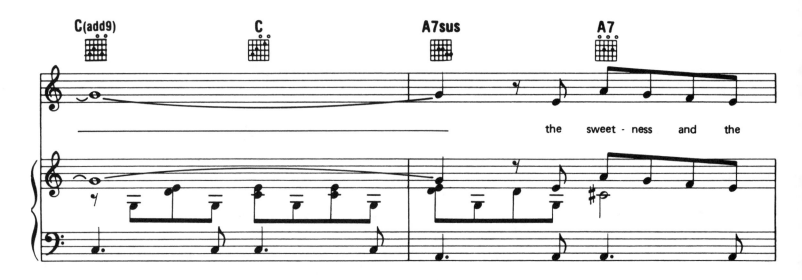

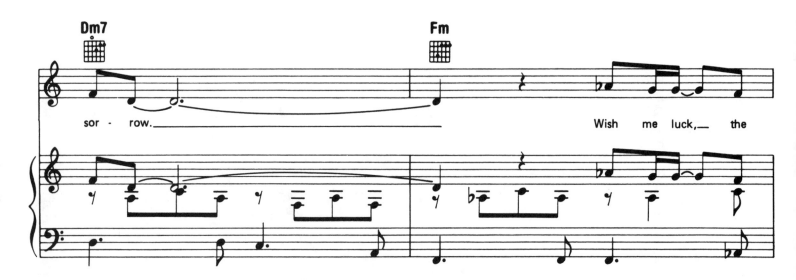

WHAT'S NEW?

Words by JOHNNY BURKE
Music by BOB HAGGART

WHAT THE WORLD NEEDS NOW IS LOVE

Lyric by HAL DAVID
Music by BURT BACHARACH

With a jazz waltz feel

What the world needs now is love, sweet love, It's the on-ly thing ___ that there's just _____ too

WHAT'LL I DO?

from MUSIC BOX REVUE OF 1924

Words and Music by
IRVING BERLIN

WHEN SUNNY GETS BLUE

Lyric by JACK SEGAL
Music by MARVIN FISHER

292

WHERE OR WHEN
from BABES IN ARMS

Words by LORENZ HART
Music by RICHARD RODGERS

WITCHCRAFT

Lyric by CAROLYN LEIGH
Music by CY COLEMAN

YOUNG AT HEART

Words by CAROLYN LEIGH
Music by JOHNNY RICHARDS

Slowly

304